PICTURE LIBRARY

BEARS

PICTURE LIBRARY

BEARS

N.S. Barrett

Franklin Watts

London   New York   Sydney   Toronto

© 1988 Franklin Watts Ltd

First published in Great Britain
    1988 by
Franklin Watts Ltd
12a Golden Square
London W1R 4BA

First published in the USA by
Franklin Watts Inc
387 Park Avenue South
New York
N.Y. 10016

First published in Australia by
Franklin Watts
14 Mars Road
Lane Cove
2066 NSW

UK ISBN: 0 86313-639-7
US ISBN: 0-531-10526-1
Library of Congress Catalog Card
Number 87-50846

Printed in Italy

Designed by
Barrett & Willard

Photographs by
Survival Anglia
Pat Morris
Ardea
Bruce Coleman Ltd/Wayne
    Lankinen (front cover)
N.S. Barrett Collection

Illustrations by
Rhoda & Robert Burns

Technical Consultant
Michael Chinery

Contents

Introduction

Bears are large animals with thick fur. They are cuddly looking creatures, and are often quite playful. But they are dangerous to people because they are very strong and attack without warning.

There are several kinds of bears. The white polar bear lives in the Arctic. Brown and black bears are found in parts of North America, Europe and Asia. The spectacled bear comes from South America.

△ A lone polar bear stands amidst the snow and ice of northern Alaska. Polar bears are able to survive the intense cold of the Arctic region because they have a thick layer of fat underneath their skin.

The naming of black and brown bears is confusing. Brown bears vary from cream colored to nearly black, and some black bears are brown.

The bear with the shaggiest fur is the sloth bear, and the smallest bear is the sun bear.

Giant pandas look like bears, but are thought to belong to a different group of animals. The koala of Australia is not a bear, even though it is sometimes called a koala bear.

△ A grizzly bear goes looking for fish while her three cubs stand on the edge of the water. Grizzlies are large brown bears of North America. They get their name from the grizzled look of their fur, which is tipped with gray.

Looking at bears

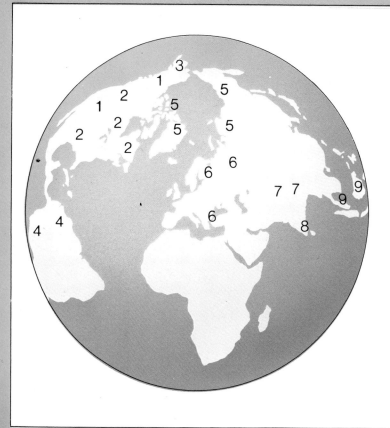

Where they live

Bears are found in many parts of the world. But no bears live in Africa or Australia. They vary in size from the huge Kodiak bear, which weighs 500 kg (1,100 lb), to the sun bear, which weighs less than 68 kg (150 lb).

1 Grizzly bear
2 American black bear
3 Kodiak bear
4 Spectacled bear
5 Polar bear
6 European brown bear
7 Himalayan black bear
8 Sloth bear
9 Sun bear

Bear sizes

Kodiak

Polar

American black

Himalayan black

Sloth

The body of a bear

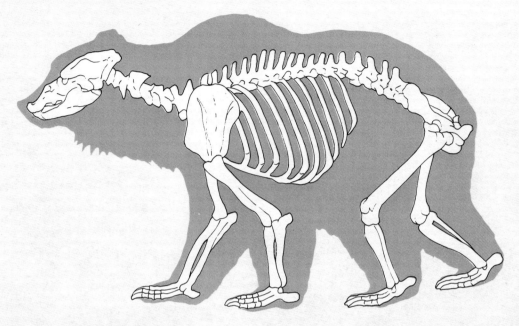

Bears are heavy animals. But underneath their long, thick fur and folds of loose skin, they are not as big as they appear. The proportions of their limbs are similar to those of human beings.

Grizzly and European brown

Spectacled   Sun

Tracking a grizzly

Bears place the whole of their feet flat on the ground when they walk or run. Because of the way they run, impressions of their hind feet are found just in front of the marks of their front feet.

Hind foot

Front foot

The life of bears

Bears do not live together except when a mother is looking after her cubs. They roam the land by themselves in search of food.

   As winter approaches, they search for a place to make their den, a cave or perhaps a hollow log. They go to sleep for most of the winter, but on warmer days might leave their den and walk around.

▽ An Asian black bear has an excellent view of the Japanese country-side as it climbs out on a high branch. Most bears are good climbers.

△ Bears are at home in the water and are very good swimmers.

▷ Having eaten a good meal, a bear enjoys an afternoon snooze in the sun.

Bears eat all kinds of food. Their diet includes meat, fish, fruit, nuts, leaves and berries.

Honey is a favorite of brown and black bears. They are protected from bee stings by their long, thick fur. They also eat ants, grubs and birds' eggs.

Bears are fast movers, and hunt small animals such as ground squirrels and mice. Polar bears live mainly on seals and whale or walrus.

△ A bear sits back to digest its meal of a deer carcass. But most bears eat far more fruit and other plant material than meat.

Bears are powerful animals. Blows from their front paws can kill a person or even a large animal such as a deer, and their long claws are dangerous weapons.

But bears are usually peaceful and steer clear of danger. They fight only when threatened, or to protect their cubs, food or home. Their greatest enemies are humans, who hunt bears and destroy forests where they live.

▽ A bear with a freshly caught salmon. Bears wade into the water to catch fish with their paws or in their mouths.

A male and female bear may live together for a few weeks. But the male wanders away and leaves the female to have cubs and raise them.

Most cubs are born while the mother is in her winter den. Bears usually have two cubs, but sometimes as many as four.

At birth, bear cubs are tiny. It is four to six weeks before they grow their fur and their eyes open.

▽ A polar bear looking after her young cub. Male bears sometimes attack young cubs and kill them. But the mother will battle fiercely to protect her young and usually fights the male off.

The mother keeps the cubs in the den for about two months. They grow quickly, and once they go outside their mother soon teaches them to find food for themselves.

Young cubs enjoy playing together. But if they annoy their mother, she might slap them or send them up a tree out of the way. Cubs usually stay with their mother for a year or more before going off to fend for themselves.

△ Two young bears enjoy a friendly wrestling match in the water. Playing helps them to keep fit and they do not hurt each other.

Brown bears

Brown bears are found in many parts of the world. They vary in size depending on the type of land they inhabit and the kind of food they eat.

Brown bears vary in color. They may be cream, gray, red or dark brown. Some are almost black, especially older bears.

△ A big, light-colored brown bear of North America.

▷ This close-up clearly shows the thick, long fur and the powerful teeth of the bear's lower jaw. The two large teeth, called canines, are used for tearing their prey.

▷ A mother grizzly scours the water for fish as her four cubs wait in line on the rocky shore.

Grizzlies are among the largest bears in the world. In North America, they live chiefly in Alaska, although there are a few in Yellowstone National Park.

Grizzlies are very much at home in the water. They are good swimmers and spend hours wading in rivers and lakes looking for fish.

The biggest brown bears are called Kodiak bears. They live in Alaska. They normally stand as tall as 2.7 m (9 ft) on their hind legs and may weigh half a ton (1,100 lb) or more.

Big brown bears grow too heavy to climb trees for food. Even so, they find plenty to eat in the forests where they live.

△ A mother Kodiak bear teaches her cub how to catch fish on a river in Alaska.

Black bears

Black bears are found in North America and in central and south-eastern Asia. They are smaller than most brown bears, standing about 1.5 m (5 ft) upright.

Black bears are common in large forested areas. They are hunted for their skins. Most states have banned or restricted hunting.

△ A black bear in a Canadian national park. Black bears are good tree climbers and fast runners.

Although they are relatively small, black bears are strong. They are curious animals and love anything sweet. For these reasons, they may be dangerous to campers, and have been known to injure or even kill people who feed them.

They sometimes damage crops and young trees, and may attack cattle and other farm animals.

△ Black bears are curious and are always on the lookout for food, especially anything sweet. Travelers in the forest must beware of them because they are stronger and more dangerous than they look.

▷ A black bear in Yellowstone National Park. Many black bears in the west of North America have brown fur.

Other kinds of bears

◁ The spectacled bear, from South America, is so-called because of the white markings around its eyes.

▷ The sloth bear of India moves slowly unless disturbed. It is sometimes called the honey bear because of its love for this food.

▽ The sun bear, or Malayan bear, lives in the forest and hunts at night. It is the smallest of all bears, standing only 1.2 m (4 ft) upright and weighing less than 70 kg (150 lb).

▷ A polar bear stands majestically against the white landscape of the Arctic ice, surveying its kingdom.

Polar bears are found mostly along the coasts of the Arctic region. They are the best swimmers of all the bears. For most of the year they eat sea animals, especially seals. They often ride ice floes searching for prey. They have pads of fur on the soles of their feet, which help them to walk on ice and keep their feet warm.

In winter, the female polar bear digs a den under the snow, which helps protect her and her newly born cubs.

The story of bears

The bear family

Bears make up the family Ursidae. They belong to an order, or subdivision, of the class of mammals called carnivores, or flesh-eaters. Their closest relatives in the animal kingdom include the pandas and raccoons, dogs and wolves, and badgers and otters.

There are several extinct types of bear, which are known from fossils found in various parts of the world. One of these, a giant cave bear, was bigger than any bear living today.

Hunting bears

People have hunted bears for thousands of years, since the Stone Age. They ate their flesh and used their skin and bones for clothing, tools and weapons.

Before the Europeans settled in North America, the Indians hunted bears, and some tribes even worshipped them as gods. Big brown bears roamed far and wide until settlers spread westward in the 1800s. The pioneers shot and trapped bears by the thousands — for their furs as well as to protect livestock.

Eskimos have always hunted polar bears. But since hunters started to travel to the Arctic to shoot polar bears for sport and for their skins, their numbers have decreased.

Cruelty to bears

Bears were first captured to provide public entertainment in Roman times, about 2,000 years ago. They were chained up and attacked by dogs or tormented by armed soldiers called gladiators.

This cruel practice of bear-baiting was revived about 900 years ago. It took place in arenas called bear gardens. It was very popular in England until it was finally outlawed in 1835.

Bears were also trained to "dance," often by cruel means. Bull and bear fighting was once popular in the United States.

The future of bears

Over the last 200 years, the numbers of bears in the world have been reduced drastically. They used to be found all over the northern parts of the world. But the invention of the rifle made them easy prey for hunters, and the destruction of forests has limited their natural habitat.

Laws to restrict hunting of bears have been introduced in North America. Even so, the

number of grizzlies has been decreasing except in Alaska and Canada, although the black bear is still flourishing. The few bears left in Europe are much prized trophies for animal hunters and only a few remain here and there.

Sloth bears and sun bears have been slaughtered senselessly for years and their natural habitats have been destroyed. They have become extinct in many areas where they previously flourished. In the last sixty or seventy years,

△ **So-called sport in California a hundred years ago. A bull is set upon a chained bear in a fight to the finish.**

the population of polar bears has been greatly reduced. But the hunting of polar bears is now strictly controlled, and numbers are increasing again.

Unless similar international laws are brought in to control the hunting of other bears, some types may well die out altogether before long.

Facts and records

Largest

The largest bear, and the largest flesh-eating animal, is the Kodiak bear, a race of brown bear found in Alaska – on Kodiak Island and on the mainland.

A fully grown male Kodiak bear averages about 2.7 m (9 ft) standing upright and weighs about 500 kg (1,100 lb). Examples weighing more than 750 kg (1,650 lb) have been known.

Polar bears are smaller on average, but one said to have weighed over 1,000 kg (2,200 lb) was killed in 1960 and mounted. The stuffed skin stands over 3.35 m (11 ft).

△ The Kodiak brown bear is the world's largest carnivore, or flesh-eating animal. It lives in parts of the US state of Alaska.

Strong swimmers

Polar bears are the fastest swimmers of all the bears. They reach speeds of 10 km/h (6 mph) in the water. With just their muzzle and eyes above the surface, they can swim for days on end.

△ Polar bears are strong swimmers, and faster in the water than any other bear.

Fastest

The black bear has been timed at speeds of 48 km/h (30 mph). Polar bears can reach speeds of 40 km/h (25 mph), even on ice. They can run fast enough to catch reindeer, but such speeds can be kept up only over very short distances.

Life span

Bears live on average from 15 to 30 years in the wild. The longest known life span for a bear in captivity is 47 years, for a brown bear in a zoo.

Glossary

Bear-baiting
The cruel practice of tormenting chained bears, once an accepted sport.

Black bear
A type of bear, smaller than most brown bears, whose color varies from black to pale brown or even nearly white.

Brown bear
A type of bear which ranges in size from the European brown bear to the very big Kodiak brown bear of Alaska and whose color varies from cream to almost black.

Canines
Strong, pointed teeth used for tearing at food.

Carnivore
A flesh-eating animal.

Den
A bear's winter home.

Extinction
When a type of animal dies out and there are no longer any living specimens.

Fossil
Any remains of ancient living things, such as bones or the impression of a paw print preserved in rock.

Grizzly bear
A type of brown bear that has fur tipped with gray.

Honey bear
Another name for the sloth bear.

Kodiak brown bear
The largest living bear, a type of brown bear found in Alaska.

Malayan bear
Another name for the sun bear.

Muzzle
The jaws and nose of an animal.

Polar bear
The white bear of the Arctic.

Sloth bear
A bear from India with flexible lips.

Spectacled bear
The only bear of South America.

Sun bear
The smallest bear, which lives in south-eastern Asia.

Index